相信你一定知道春节、元旦、中秋节。你知道清明节吗？

清明节在每年的四月四日到四月六日之间,是中国的传统节日。

　　中国的大多数传统节日都以合家团圆为主。不同于中国的其他节日，清明节的主要传统活动是扫墓。

在清明节这一天，人们会去墓地为去世的亲人扫墓，表达对亲人的思念。

扫墓时，人们通常会带上一些食物或者花。人们也会和亲人说说话，希望亲人能听到他们的思念。

清明节又叫"踏青节",所以去郊外春游也是清明节的一个传统活动。

　　清明节时正是春天。树绿了，花开了，到处都是一片春回大地的美好<u>景象</u>。老老少少一家人一起去郊外春游，感受大自然的美丽，再好不过了。

　　清明节也是一年中雨水比较多的时候，所以很多地方也有在清明节种树的习俗。种下一棵棵树木，代表着人们对大自然的热爱。

现在你知道清明节的传统和习俗了,今年的清明节,你会去扫墓吗?你会去踏青吗?你也会种一棵"清明树"吗?

Glossary

	Pinyin	English Definition
相信	xiāng xìn	to believe
元旦	yuán dàn	New Year's Day
传统	chuán tǒng	tradition
合家团圆	hé jiā tuán yuán	the whole family to come together
扫墓	sǎo mù	to sweep a grave and pay one's respects to the dead person
墓地	mù dì	cemetery
去世	qù shì	to pass way
表达	biǎo dá	to express
思念	sī niàn	to miss
通常	tōng cháng	usually
或者	huò zhě	or
踏青	tà qīng	spring hike season around Qingming festival
郊外	jiāo wài	countryside
景象	jǐng xiàng	scenery
习俗	xí sú	custom
代表	dài biǎo	to represent

Copyright © 2022 by Level Learning INC.

All rights reserved. No part of this book in whole or part may be reproduced without written permission from the publisher

Author: Jingyao Qi, Level Learning

Simplified Chinese Edition

- This is the last page of this book. -

www.ingramcontent.com/pod-product-compliance
Lightning Source LLC
Chambersburg PA
CBHW041217070526
44583CB00001B/23